The Buddha's Marketing Blueprint

Strategies for Conscious Business

Table of Contents

Chapter 1. Introduction

Dive into the wisdom of the ages with our unique Special Report, "The Buddha's Marketing Blueprint: Strategies for Conscious Business." This insightful guide finds harmony between ancient wisdom and modern business practices, offering a fresh take on corporate strategies in today's environmentally and socially conscious marketplace. With engaging language and enlightening examples, our special report takes you on an exciting journey, unveiling how Buddha's timeless teachings can truly revolutionize your business practices. Prepare to ignite your curiosity, enhance your business acumen, and generate success with love and mindfulness. With "The Buddha's Marketing Blueprint," success is but a conscious choice away!

Chapter 2. The Intersection of Buddhism and Business: An Introduction

Buddhism, a global religion established some 2,500 years ago by Siddhartha Gautama, or the Buddha, holds profound wisdom painstakingly gathered and understood over millennia. By investigating these primal teachings, we can unearth profound strategies and philosophies beneficial to contemporary businesses.

2.1. The Origin of Buddhism

The spiritual journey towards Buddhism began in northern India, where Prince Siddhartha Gautama sought enlightenment to escape the endless cycle of suffering represented by birth, death, and rebirth. Following years of ascetic practices and meditation under a Bodhi tree, he attained enlightenment and transformed into the Buddha - the 'Awakened One.' His revealed wisdom, encapsulated in the Four Noble Truths and the Eightfold Path, help alleviate suffering and guide people towards enlightenment. This comprehensive moral and ethical system, though religious in nature, conceals essential business lessons on decision-making, leadership, compassion, and mindfulness.

2.2. Basics of Buddhist Philosophy

To approach Buddhism's intersection with business, we must initially comprehend Buddhism's foundational tenets. The Four Noble Truths depict life's inherent suffering, its origins, the possibility of its cessation, and the path leading to it, whereas the Eightfold Path lays out moral conduct, concentration, and wisdom. These values include right view, intention, speech, action, livelihood, effort, mindfulness, and concentration, which provide useful, ethical guidelines for business practices too.

2.3. Buddhism and Business Ethics

Examining Buddhist principles from a business perspective, ethics underscores every line of thought.

Right Intention, for instance, emphasizes sincerity, kindness, and compassion, which are tremendously instrumental in fostering a positive corporate culture and client relationships. Companies that genuinely invest in clients and employees often enjoy higher engagement and loyalty, leading to sustained growth and success.

Dissimilar to intentions, Right Action underscores the importance of ethical conduct. In the business context, upholding moral standards helps establish corporate integrity and accountability, key factors for garnering stakeholder trust and fostering lasting business relationships.

2.4. The Role of Mindfulness in Business

In recent years, mindfulness, another prime Buddhist tenet, has stormed into business best practices. Rooted in Buddhist meditation practices, mindfulness revolves around being attentively present in the moment, leading to focused work, enhanced engagement, and improved interpersonal relationships.

Mindful leaders encourage more open, transparent communication, fostering an inclusive atmosphere where employees feel valued and heard. Moreover, teams practising mindfulness display heightened creativity and improved problem-solving capabilities—critical elements of organizational success.

2.5. Compassionate Leadership

Buddha's teachings emphasized compassion, an element vital for proficient leadership. Compassionate leaders, cognizant of employees' needs and sentiments, foster a supportive environment conducive to high productivity and morale. This facet correlates with the Buddhist concept of interconnectedness, reminding us of our common humanity and the importance of collective success.

2.6. Buddha and Operational Wisdom

Buddhism promotes impartiality. When incorporated into business, this principle encourages fair and equitable practices, contributing to a congenial work culture. Furthermore, Buddhism draws attention towards impermanence — the concept that all things are transient and ever-changing. Companies who recognize this propensity towards change can maintain flexibility in their strategies and adapt swiftly to ever-changing market trends, thereby gaining a significant competitive edge.

In conclusion, the crossroads of Buddhism and business may appear unusual at first glance. However, the Buddha's teachings, emphasizing ethical conduct, mindfulness, compassionate leadership, and collective success, are pragmatically applicable and beneficial for businesses. Unearthing these wisdom gems from the world's fourth-largest religion, businesses can imbibe imperishable guidelines that promote enduring success alongside societal goodwill. Therefore, successful business leadership doesn't necessitate choosing between profit and ethics or growth and compassion. It's merely about discovering the right balance, and Buddhism has much to teach us in that regard. Upon discerning these wisdom nuggets, one can commence an enlightening journey to corporate success with love, mindfulness, and compassion.

By integrating principles of Buddhism - compassion, mindfulness, and ethics - into contemporary corporate practices, we can reenvision, reshape, and revolutionize businesses towards becoming conscious entities, serving not just shareholders, but also society at large.

Chapter 3. The Four Noble Truths: Understanding and Overcoming Business Suffering

Examining business challenges through the lens of The Four Noble Truths, a fundamental framework in Buddhism, we can decipher a path to alleviate certain forms of "corporate suffering." These truths: the reality of suffering, the cause of suffering, the end of suffering, and the path leading to the end of suffering, can be related to business problems. Analogously, we speak of business suffering, its source, its cessation, and the pathway to its resolution.

3.1. The Reality of Business Suffering

Buddha taught that to live is to suffer (dukkha), and in business this might translate to the inescapable challenges that enterprises face. This could be financial shortfalls, employee turnover, or even an economic recession. Businesses are subjected to regular trials and tribulations.

Suffering in business isn't solely limited to monumental events but is also associated with day-to-day challenges. It may be an employee causing disruption, a customer complaint that threatens your reputation, or an unexpected delay in the supply chain. Accepting this reality is the first step towards addressing these problems wisely and with understanding.

3.2. The Origin of Business Suffering

With the acknowledgement of the reality of business suffering, we move onto the second truth of Buddha – the cause, or origin, of suffering (samudaya).

The Buddha propounds that the root cause of suffering is attachment, desire, or thirst (trishna). In business, this is analogous to the constant pursuit of more – more clients, more profit, more growth. While aspirations to grow are not innately negative, it becomes a problem when waged without consideration for sustainability or societal impact. This insatiable desire often leads to stress, burnout, and ethical compromises.

Business suffering also originates from clinging to outdated business models or strategies. The refusal to diversify, innovate or adapt to change, can lead to stagnation or even bankruptcy. Lack of conflict resolution, sticking to toxic workplace cultures, or choosing short-term gains over long-term sustainability are other potential sources of business suffering.

3.3. The Cessation of Business Suffering

The third Noble Truth teaches us that suffering can cease (nirodha) when we let go of our desires and attachments. In the world of business, this suggests that solutions can be found in the root causes we just discussed.

By adjusting your perspective and implementing mindful business strategies, you can alleviate suffering. Prioritizing mental health in the workplace, business sustainability, and ethical conduct can allow you to break free from the endless cycle of desire and dissatisfaction.

For example, adopting conscious employment practices like offering flexible hours, positive work environments, and emphasis on work-life balance can reduce employee dissatisfaction and turnover. Moreover, a business model emphasizing sustainability can not only drive long-term profits but also improve public perception and customer loyalty.

3.4. The Eightfold Path: Leading to the Cessation of Suffering

The fourth and final Noble Truth offers a path (magga) to end suffering: the Eightfold Path. It outlines areas for self-improvement, which can be interpreted as an eight-step process to better business practices.

1. Right Understanding: Understanding your business's true purpose, beyond just profits.

2. Right Thought: Implementing ethical decision making in all business operations.

3. Right Speech: Encouraging open, honest, and respectful communication.

4. Right Action: Ensuring all business actions are ethical and considerate of societal impact.

5. Right Livelihood: Maintaining fair employment practices and sustainable business models.

6. Right Effort: Continually striving for improvement and innovation.

7. Right Mindfulness: Staying aware and observant of business process and its impacts, internally and externally.

8. Right Concentration: Focusing on achieving business objectives without compromising on ethical standards and sustainability.

By adhering to these principles, businesses can consciously strive to alleviate suffering. It's all about aiming for success, not solely characterized by profit, but by its impact on employees, consumers, the environment, and society at large.

Through the translation of The Four Noble Truths into a business context, we can gain wisdom and guidance to revisit our corporate strategies. Emphasizing consciousness in our businesses prepares us to face challenges with wisdom and compassion, making not just our businesses, but our world a better place. Welcome to the era of the Buddha's marketing blueprint, where success is defined not by the heights achieved, but by the depth of your business's wisdom and compassion.

Chapter 4. The Noble Eightfold Path: Ethical Guidelines for Conscious Businesses

To fully grasp the transformative potential of Buddha's teachings in the business realm, we must first come to understand The Noble Eightfold Path — a central component of these teachings that provides a holistic paradigm for ethical, sustainable, and human-centric operations. This path is comprised of Right Understanding, Right Intent, Right Speech, Right Action, Right Livelihood, Right Effort, Right Mindfulness, and Right Concentration. Each directive serves as a foundation to guide business strategies and inspire truly conscious decision-making.

4.1. Right Understanding

The first element, Right Understanding, challenges us to grasp the realities of our business world and comprehend the effect of our actions therein. Understanding is about awareness, about seeing the total picture, about accepting the truths of interdependence, uncertainty, and constant change in business. It also means understanding the ways in which conscious marketing can make a significant difference to your business, to your customers, and ultimately to the world.

In our current era, we can apply this principle by undertaking detailed market research, studying latest trends, and attentively analysing our business's social and environmental impact. The more we understand, the better we can strategize to mitigate any negative impacts while enhancing the positives. The key here is to integrate a constant cycle of learning and adaptation in the way we conduct business.

4.2. Right Intent

Right Intent, the second element, means aligning our objectives with ethical standards and the greater good. Conscious businesses are not simply about making profits — they are about creating value for multiple stakeholders: employees, customers, the community, the environment, and yes, the shareholders as well.

For a business, Right Intent translates into having a mission statement and set of values that are rooted in ethical, corporal social responsibility, and sustainable practices. It means setting goals not just for financial growth, but for societal and environmental improvement. It encourages empathy towards all stakeholders and fosters an underlying intention to benefit all involved.

4.3. Right Speech

In business, Right Speech means honest, clear and empathetic communication. It's about the authenticity of your marketing messages, the honesty in your sales pitches, the clarity of your product descriptions, and the respectfulness of your customer service interactions.

Inherent in this principle is the understanding that words hold power. Negative or misleading communication can damage a company's reputation and customer relationships. On the other hand, respectful and authentic speech can build trust, loyalty, and positive brand recognition. Conscious businesses practice right speech through establishing clear, open, and mutually respectful communication channels with all stakeholders.

4.4. Right Action

Right Action means conducting business operations in an ethical, lawful, and responsible manner. It's about ensuring your supply chain is fair, your working conditions are satisfactory, your business practices are transparent, and your impact on the environment is as minimal as possible.

To implement Right Action, businesses must establish strong ethical guidelines in their operations and abide by those standards consistently. They must also engage with suppliers and partners that uphold the same ethical values. Right Action is about being a good corporate citizen and embodies the very foundation of corporate ethics.

4.5. Right Livelihood

Right Livelihood is the call for businesses to engage in commerce that benefits not just stakeholders, but also society at large, and does no harm. It propagates that the core of one's business—the products or services it offers—should align with the principles of fairness, sustainability, and positive contribution.

Applying this in today's world, businesses must exclusively deal in products or services that do good or at least do no harm. For a business to truly tread the path of conscious commerce, it's essential that they examine their fundamental offerings and ensure they are providing a considerate livelihood for all involved.

4.6. Right Effort

Right Effort refers to the unwavering commitment to ethical business conduct, environmental protections, and social progression. It's a long-term dedication to improving, learning, and growing consciously as a business.

To apply Right Effort, a business must create a systematic approach to routinely review its policies, initiatives, and practices against its ethical, environmental, and social goals. It requires continuous learning, adapting, and gradually moving towards improved practices that increase the positive impact while decreasing the negative.

4.7. Right Mindfulness

Right Mindfulness, in business, means being acutely aware of the effects of our actions on stakeholders, society, and the environment. It's about making mindful decisions — decisions that are not driven by mere short-term profit but take into account the broader implications on all stakeholders.

It's about embracing an empathic approach towards employees, implementing eco-friendly manufacturing processes, considering the societal impact of a product, or the way an advertising campaign could affect the mental health of consumers. Mindfulness in business fosters thoughtful business practices that facilitate well-balanced growth for everyone involved.

4.8. Right Concentration

Right Concentration is about focused, diligent and consistent practice of these guidelines in all aspects of business. Just as a meditator concentrates on their breath, a business must focus on maintaining these ethical paths in all its actions and decisions.

Contained in this are practices like regular ethical audits, company-wide mindfulness training, and continuous focus on conscious business practices. It's not enough to simply understand or want to implement these ethical guidelines — concentration on their application is what brings significant transformation in business practices and outcomes.

The employment of Buddha's Noble Eightfold Path can truly revolutionize the way businesses operate, leading them down the path of conscious, sustainable, and holistic success. For a business world often regarded as driven by profit, integrating these principles not only provides a more humane and ethical approach but also offers a unique competitive advantage. It's time we realize that success, compassion, and ethical conduct in business are not mutually exclusive but can instead reinforce each other, creating an incredibly potent formula for sustainable prosperity.

Chapter 5. Mindfulness: The Powerful Tool for Effective Marketing Strategy

Understanding the power of mindfulness in the world of marketing begins with a simple yet profound premise: the absolute present moment holds an unmatched wealth of potential. This key axiom forms the basis for any effective marketing strategy.

5.1. The Basics of Mindfulness

Used widely in a multiplicity of contexts, mindfulness refers to the psychological process of deliberately bringing one's attention to what is happening in the present, without any form of judgment. This process creates a pure awareness or wakefulness that allows us to be fully present and to understand deeply our own experiences and that of others.

Conscientious marketers recognize being mindfully present—having conscious awareness—can facilitate deeper connections with consumers. By understanding consumers' experiences, their wants, needs, and fears, marketers can create strategies that are both authentic and genuinely helpful.

5.2. Leveraging Mindfulness in Marketing

Marketers often operate in an environment of perennial flux. To navigate this, the first stepping stone involves attuning themselves to their environment consciously. By applying mindfulness, marketers can tune into subtle signals from the marketplace, paving the way for innovative strategies.

We see the likes of giants like Apple, Google, and other successful businesses employing mindfulness to create products and services that resonate deeply with their users. They use the insights gained from being consciously aware to continuously meet and exceed the expectations of their clientele.

The paramount step, however, is to translate these insights into actions. For instance, paying heed to what consumers really value, not just what they buy, can create avenues for businesses to engage on a more personal level. Consequently, this leads to the creation of products or services that not only fulfill the customers' immediate needs but also tend to their overall well-being.

5.3. Mindful Marketing in an Age of Distraction

In an era where consumers are bombarded with a plethora of marketing messages, it is essential for businesses to stand out, not by being the loudest, but by being the most relevant. This is where mindfulness comes into play.

Mindfulness helps businesses understand the context in which their consumers operate. By deeply understanding the complexities of consumers' lives, mindful marketers create strategies that align with their values and serve their unique needs.

For example, by contextualizing messages and coupling them with a deep understanding of the consumer, businesses can create incredibly personalized marketing strategies. Instead of just another marketing message, they become solutions to real-world problems.

5.4. Mindfulness and Consumer Relationships

In the relationship between businesses and consumers, mindfulness can play a decisive role. A mindful business won't just seek to sell at all costs; instead, it will seek to understand and fulfill consumers' needs effectively and compassionally.

Such a principle-driven approach ensures long-term customer loyalty and significantly boosts business reputation. This not only benefits the business in terms of profit and growth but also contributes positively to the broader community, thus helping fulfill the company's social responsibilities.

5.5. The Outcome of Mindful Marketing

Embedding mindfulness at the core of marketing strategies undoubtedly takes time, but the benefits reaped are well worth it. As a business becomes more in-tune with its consumer base's needs, it creates avenues for authentic connection, ensuring that their products or services are not just meeting immediate needs but enhancing their users' overall quality of life.

These insights also steer businesses toward creating more relevant, targeted marketing messages. By actively listening and taking note of consumers' needs and wants, businesses can deliver tailored experiences that not only resonate but also create a sense of trust.

The ultimate result matches what Buddha's teachings have always espoused: sustainable success fused with enhanced well-being for all. In the grand scheme of things, the completeness of a 'win-win' situation arises - the business thrives, as does its consumer base, and in turn, the broader community.

Given these potent benefits, it's unarguable that mindfulness can be a powerful tool for a transformative marketing strategy. By fostering mindfulness, businesses can construct bridges of understanding, connection, empathy, and trust with consumers. This paradigm-shift, in the long run, will redefine the meaning of business success, recasting it as a harmonious blend of profitability, social responsibility, and customer satisfaction.

Chapter 6. Right Livelihood: Transforming Corporate Vision and Mission

Rooted in the Eightfold Path taught by the Buddha, Right Livelihood focuses on choosing a way of life that does not harm others and is congruous with one's principles and values. Transforming this concept into the business world, it will refine your corporate vision and mission, yielding a business that operates consciously and contributes positively to society and the environment.

Today's business environment, dominated by capitalism and competition, often overlooks the importance of a 'right livelihood.' Transitioning from traditional, profit-centric business practices to mindful, positive-impact driven ones won't be easy, but the long-term rewards are immense.

6.1. Applying Right Livelihood to Business Practices

In business, Right Livelihood starts with the realization that all corporate actions have consequences. The choice of what to produce, sell, or provide as a service carries significant weight. A company must choose its offerings wisely, assuring they do not inflict harm on people, animals, or the environment.

What your organization chooses to trade or the services it chooses to offer are interconnected with your corporate vision and mission. Ensuring your products or services align with principles of Right Livelihood will transform your business into a force for positive change, creating a sustainable and socially-responsible brand in the process.

6.2. Crafting the Corporate Vision and Mission

The foundation of your entire operation is your corporate vision and mission. A well-defined vision and mission provide direction, mission, and a sense of purpose. They form the backbone on which the company's strategic plans, goals, and corporate culture are built.

Your company vision, in essence, should encompasses the ultimate goal your business is aiming to achieve. Is it merely about making profits, or do you aspire to contribute to societal and environmental wellbeing? What is the lasting legacy you want to create?

On the other hand, your mission statement defines what your business does and how it fulfills its purpose. It should reflect the essence of Right Livelihood by addressing who your company helps, what it does, and how it seeks to make a difference.

Remember, a distinct mission and vision not only guide your company's trajectory but also resonate with conscious consumers, thus enhancing your brand reputation.

6.3. Mindfully Defining Your Business Objectives

Right Livelihood encourages conscious decision-making, which applies to defining your business objectives too. Objectives should not get constrained to profit-making. They should encompass the broader impact of your business activity on your employees, customers, stakeholders, and the environment.

Creating sustainable objectives requires adequate consideration of four key factors: financial, environmental, societal, and operational. By mindfully defining objectives considering these four pillars, your business will operate more responsibly and sustainably.

6.4. Integrating Right Livelihood: A Practical Approach

1. Awareness and Assessment: Scrutinize your existing business practices, evaluate your products or services, supply chain, and corporate culture. Analyze if they align with the principles of Right Livelihood, and pinpoint areas that need rectification.

2. Redefine Vision and Mission: Use your assessment's insights to redefine your corporate vision and mission with principles of Right Livelihood at the core. Assure they articulate your commitment to conscious business practices.

3. Align Objectives to Mission and Vision: Once your mission and vision align with Right Livelihood, it's time to ensure that your business objectives reflect the same. Align operations, services, and even marketing strategies to your conscious business vision.

4. Engage and Communicate: Transparency is crucial in a conscious business. Keep your organization abreast with the transition and communicate clearly the changes and their implications. Foster an organizational culture that encourages Right Livelihood.

5. Review and Evolve: Implementing Right Livelihood is not one-time. It's an ongoing process. Evaluate your practices regularly to assess progress, address shortcomings, and adapt to changing scenarios.

In conclusion, transforming a corporate vision and mission with Right Livelihood as a guiding principle is a powerful step towards rising as a conscious business. The shift towards such mindful business practices reflects a company's commitment to societal and environmental well-being, leading to lasting success and a legacy that goes beyond monetary gains. Embrace Right Livelihood, and witness the transformation of your business and, indeed, your world.

Chapter 7. Karma in Business: The Role of Cause and Effect in Marketing

In the realm of conscious business, understanding hard facts and figures alone is not adequate. We must also dive into the esoteric, such as karma - the universal principle of cause and effect. Karma, a concept deeply rooted in the Buddhist philosophy, has poignant implications for modern marketing strategies.

7.1. Ancient Wisdom: Understanding Karma

In simple terms, karma relates to the natural law of 'sow and reap.' It preaches that every action, be it physical or mental, generates an energy that will return to us in kind. Translating this to a business context, every action we undertake as a company—marketing strategies, customer interactions, product development—propagates a ripple, the effects of which return to touch us.

This notion of karma encourages businesses to be mindful and strive toward ensuring that the actions they initiate are guided by wisdom, compassion, and a deeper sense of purpose.

7.2. Applying Karma in Marketing

Effective marketing today is about resonance, not imposition. It's not about pushing a product but about delivering genuine value to the customer, thereby creating a positive relationship that encourages reciprocation and loyalty.

1) Mindfulness in Marketing: Promoting products in a way that

respects the customer and their needs, rather than exploiting their vulnerabilities, generates positive marketing karma. This can establish a brand image of sincerity and reliability, leading customers to be more responsive and loyal.

2) Taking Responsibility: Businesses must recognize the good and adverse effects that their activities can cause. The responsibility lies with businesses to assess the impact of their actions and rectify their course if needed. This principle finds new significance in today's green-conscious market, where the success of a product is also measured by its environmental footprint.

3) Positive Customer Experiences: Create products and experiences that genuinely enhance the customer's life. A satisfied customer contributes positively to a company's karma pool, helping it earn reputation, trust, and loyalty.

7.3. The Cycle of Business Karma

Every business wants to sow the seeds of success. This necessitates cognizance of the cycle of business karma: input (intention and action), process (energy set in motion), and outcome (effect).

1) Input: Before launching any marketing campaign, examine its underlying intention. Is it to merely boost sales or provide customers with real value? A clear intention forms the seed of karmic energy.

2) Process: The action sets the energy in motion. This could be an inclusive ad campaign, a customer-friendly return policy, or an eco-friendly product.

3) Outcome: The generated effect is the return of the karmic energy spawned by the intention and its subsequent action.

Here, it's essential to note that the effects of karmic energy may not be immediate. Just as seeds sown today take time to grow and produce fruits, the energy initiated due to a business's actions may take time before it shows noticeable outcomes.

7.4. Ethical Business: The Path of Right Action

Buddhism teaches the importance of the path of 'right action'. This concept extends beyond avoiding outright harm. In the context of business choices, right action implies decisions that are ethically sound, environmentally sustainable, and focused on long-term value.

With increasing competition and the ever-present drive for growth, there can be a temptation to veer from the 'right action'. However, businesses need to remember that while these actions might bring temporary success, in the long run, they may tarnish the brand image and trust, bringing negative business karma.

Choosing right action in business practices and marketing strategies preserves the integrity of the brand. Thus, ethical marketing not only contributes to positive karma but also promotes sustainable growth.

7.5. Conclusion: The Karmic Influencer

Embracing the concept of karma can revolutionize the way businesses strategize their actions. By focusing on generating positive karmic outcomes, businesses can forge a deeper bond with their customers, evolve their brand persona, and carve a path of sustainable and conscious growth.

The Buddha's marketing blueprint instructs us to align business strategies with age-old wisdom. Through karma, we're enlightened to the vast interconnectedness of actions and their effects. Understanding this can be the key to creating marketing strategies that not only reap monetary success but also sow seeds of social and environmental positivity. In a world driving toward mindful consumption, there's no better time than now to reconsider marketing from the karmic perspective. A shift toward conscious business and marketing practices today will echo in the realm of sustained success tomorrow.

Chapter 8. Impermanence and Adaptability: Staying Relevant in a Changing Market

In the teachings of Buddha, the concept of Impermanence, known as Anicca in Pali, is a foundational principle. It means that all conditioned phenomena in the world are constantly changing, in a state of flux. Whether it's atoms, humans, stars, or markets, every entity is intrinsically transient and continuously evolving. This chapter aims to harness this profound wisdom and apply it to the business realm, predominantly on the notions of adaptability, resilience, and innovativeness, with the final goal of maintaining relevance in a fluctuating marketplace.

8.1. Form is Emptiness, Emptiness is Form

In the renowned Heart Sutra, there resides a profound phrase that we can apply to our discussion, "Form is emptiness, and emptiness is form." It implies that the forms we see around us are not permanent, they come into being due to certain conditions. Once those conditions change, the form changes too. This is highly relevant in the context of businesses and the market they operate in.

Companies often start by providing a product or service that addresses a specific need in the marketplace. Over time, they develop a business model, a set of practices, and a culture all built around it. However, with the concept of impermanence at play, market conditions change, technologies evolve, and customer needs shift. Thus, organizations that strictly identify themselves with a particular form (product, service, or even a business model) may find their relevance eroding.

The wisdom here is to perceive the 'form' of one's business as 'emptiness,' meaning it is adaptable, subject to change, and should not be firmly attached. It does not undermine the importance of a product, service, or business model, but it emphasizes the flexibility of transforming these 'forms' as per the changing landscape.

8.2. Keeping Abreast of the Current and Future Trends

Impermanence, by its very nature, is about evolution and progress. In business, this translates to staying updated with the present market trends and, even more importantly, looking forward and planning for future movements. Active engagement with customers, continuous market research, keeping an eye on global developments, and agile decision-making systems are some of the means to adapt to the changing tides.

However, merely staying updated isn't enough. Just as Right Mindfulness is a key factor to enlightenment in Buddhism, Mindful Forecasting is critical to business survival and growth. It is about being alert to the subtle shifts, nuanced changes, and emerging patterns in your industry, thereby enabling necessary transformations in the 'form,' well in advance of the dramatic shifts in the market landscape.

8.3. Embracing Change: Leveraging Digital Disruptions

Another important dimension of applying the concept of Anicca to business is the active embrace of change. Digitization and technology-driven changes are the current major disruptors. From

AI-infused customer service to blockchain-driven contracts, from mobile-first services to big data analytics, the digital disruptions sweeping across sectors are both a challenge and an opportunity.

Businesses that view these as threats to their established models struggle with the change. However, those seeing it as an opportunity - viewing their 'form' as 'empty,' can devise innovative offerings, streamline operations, enhance customer experiences, and even create entirely new market segments. It's not about abandoning the past completely; rather, it's about adapting the strengths from the past to the present needs and future opportunities.

8.4. Thriving amid Uncertainty: Cultivating Resilience

Uncertainty is an inherent part of a rapidly changing market environment. How a company responds to uncertainty significantly determines its longevity and success. One key strategy is to cultivate resilience. Just as Buddhism emphasizes the Middle Path, avoiding extreme reactions and maintaining equanimity, businesses too can learn to neither overly panic nor become overly complacent in the face of market ambiguity.

Building reserves, enhancing the diversity in offerings, decentralizing decision-making, enabling a culture of innovation, and promoting lean and flexible operations are some strategies to cultivate resilience. It helps companies keep a steady hand in turbulent waters, enabling them to maneuver skillfully to overcome obstacles and seize opportunities.

8.5. Impermanence as Innovation

Innovation, often seen as a cornerstone of business success, naturally aligns with the concept of impermanence. If everything is transitory and continuously evolving, innovation is the business world's translation of this reality. But we must approach innovation with a broad mindset far beyond simply churning out new products or services.

Innovation should permeate every facet of an organization, from operations to customer service, from hiring strategies to company culture. Encouraging experimentation, accepting failures as learning points, rewarding creative thinking, fostering diversity, and maintaining an open culture are crucial to cultivate a broader ethos of innovation, helping businesses to continuously transform and remain relevant.

The Buddha's teachings of impermanence provide multifaceted wisdom for companies to stay relevant in the complex, ever-changing marketplace. By deeply understanding and applying the above principles of 'form is emptiness,' staying abreast of trends, embracing change, cultivating resilience, and fostering pervasive innovation, businesses can transform impermanence from a daunting challenge into a powerful catalyst for adaptability and continuous evolution. The potential benefits, ranging from improved services to pioneering breakthroughs, are vast and impactful, reflecting the modern-day relevance of Buddha's ancient wisdom.

Chapter 9. The Middle Path: Balancing Profit and Purpose

Historically, the dichotomy of profit versus purpose has long been an area of contention for businesses worldwide. Reaching a point of equilibrium, where both components harmoniously meld together, often appears elusive, but it wasn't for Siddhartha Gautama, better known as Buddha. The principle of 'The Middle Path,' one of Buddha's most cherished teachings, offers insights we can use to balance profit and purpose in our businesses.

9.1. The Concept of the Middle Path

The Middle Path, also known as the Noble Eightfold Path, is a guide to ethical and mental development with the aim to free individuals from attachments and delusions, ultimately leading to understanding, peace, and enlightenment. In the world of business, enlightenment can symbolize the achieving of our desired objectives, whether they are higher revenues, wider market domination, or an elevated brand image. We can understand attachments and delusions as those business practices that are short-sighted, unethical, or unsustainable.

It's imperative to comprehend that The Middle Path doesn't necessitate a compromise between profit and purpose. Instead, it is an enlightened approach to business that appreciates the essentialness of both elements, operating in harmony with each other.

9.2. Profit Interpreted in the Middle Path

Buddha never repudiated the significance of prosperity. In fact, Dana, or the virtue of giving, is a foundational aspect of Buddhism. Without resources - a proxy for profit in commerce - one cannot partake in Dana and contribute to the welfare of others.

Here, profit symbolizes the vital resource that fuels the engine of business, drives innovation, and facilitates growth. Without it, survival in competitive marketplaces would be unimaginable. However, the Middle Path encourages us to view profit not as an ultimate destination, but as a tool, a means to make positive impacts.

In the context of our businesses, this implies pursuing profits in a way that respects our stakeholders, the environment, the rules of the market, and respects our fundamental vision or purpose.

9.3. Purpose Interpreted in the Middle Path

The other side of this equation is purpose, called 'Dhamma' in Buddhism. Intrinsically linked to ethical and just practices, the Dhamma can be interpreted as business ethics and purpose. The Middle Path commends those who respect Dhamma, emphasizing principles such as right understanding, right livelihood, and right efforts, all tying into ethical and responsible behavior.

What does this mean for our businesses? A clear-cut purpose gives our company a unique sense of identity and direction. It helps differentiate us from competitors, strengthens customer relations, and positively influences our brand image. This purpose can include ethical considerations such as social responsibilities, employee welfare, environmental sustainability, and more.

9.4. Balancing Through Right Action

Buddha suggested that balancing these factors - profit and purpose - lies in what is known as 'Right Actions,' an essential Tenet of the Middle Path. For businesses, 'Right Action' proposes that our business practices should be ethical, just, and humane.

In real-world context, 'Right Action' might mean implementing fair trade practices, ensuring worker safety, paying equitable wages, or investing in sustainable technology. These actions fulfill the dual purpose of helping companies stay socially and ethically responsible while also aiding in revenue and profit generation. They help build trust and loyalty among consumers, strengthening the brand's position in a competitive market.

9.5. Road to Balance: Practical Strategies

The Middle Path isn't just philosophical talk; it encourages practical, actionable strategies. You can initiate policies that bring benefits to the wider community, and at the same time, help generate better financial results for your business. Some strategies may include environmentally friendly initiatives, supporting local communities, ethical supply chains, and fostering employee development programs.

9.6. Case Study: Conscious Companies Walking the Middle Path

Several companies have successfully harmonized profit and purpose, embodying the Middle Path philosophy in their core strategies. To gain a better understanding of this balance, let's explore some of these businesses in detail.

To bring the Middle Path doctrine to life, we can inspect companies like Patagonia, Ben & Jerry's, and The Body Shop. These market powerhouses are influential examples of enterprises prioritizing profit and purpose equally. They have managed to strike a balance that ensures their financial success while making significant positive impacts on their stakeholders and the environment.

The Middle Path, therefore, is not simply a philosophical concept but a pragmatic one to apply in today's vibrant and fluctuating business landscape. The attempt to balance profit and purpose through the Middle Path can configure a business strategy that encourages steady growth while promoting an enlightened and conscious approach to marketing and business practices.

Small or large, at any stage of maturation, a business can immerse itself in the Middle Path's wisdom. It affirms that profitable operations and adherence to a purpose - to ethical practices and social responsibility – are not only feasible together but can also create a synergy, further bolstering the business's potential to enjoy enduring success and make a meaningful difference. The Middle Path promises a prosperous harmonized continuum where profit and purpose are no longer at opposite ends but poised in perfect symmetry.

Chapter 10. Interdependence and Networking: Building Sustainable Business Relationships

In the realm of Buddha's teachings, all life and existence is interconnected. This concept, often referred to as interdependence or dependent origination, carries immense implications for the business world, especially in the aspect of networking and alliance-building.

Embracing the principle of interdependence means acknowledging that your business does not thrive in isolation but is an integral part of a complex ecosystem. This understanding can create the bedrock of sustainable business relationships and partnerships based on mutual benefit, generosity, trust, and understanding.

10.1. Setting the Stage: Mutual Dependencies in the Corporate World

In an intricately connected world, every business transaction is a crucial strand, weaving together the complicated web of corporate existence. A small vendor providing necessary components for a tech giant, a financial firm granting loans to a burgeoning startup, or a transport company ensuring the timely delivery of products, each is as essential to the tapestry of business as the other. The corporate world follows a mutual dependency model where success is deeply intertwined and cannot exist in a void.

The very first step to leverage these dependencies to your advantage requires acknowledging their existence and importance. Once recognized, the connections can be nurtured, resulting in a robust network that allows for exponential growth and success. This, however, necessitates an shift in perspective: switching from a view of competition and isolation to one of collaboration and interconnected functionality.

10.2. The Art of Building Relationships: Listening and Understanding

Taking the first step towards establishing sustainable business relationships requires a nod towards another of Buddha's teachings: the importance of Right Understanding and Right Intent. Building relationships is not a one-time transaction but an ongoing process that flourishes with time, trust, and understanding.

To network effectively, we must listen actively and empathize with others. By understanding their interests, goals, and struggles, we can identify opportunities for collaboration that result in mutual benefit, thereby aligning with the principle of interdependence. Putting ourselves in others' shoes helps build trust and respect, instilling in others the feeling of being understood and valued – a cornerstone of strong, lasting relationships.

10.3. The Concept of 'Dana': Generosity in Business

'Dana' or generosity is one of the ten 'paramitas' (virtues) that Buddha stressed. By viewing business relationships through the lens of 'dana,' we promote benevolence over selfishness in the corporate sphere. To cultivate generosity, seek to provide value in your interactions – your contributions could range from expert advice to resources that help them excel in their business.

In the long run, 'dana' creates an ecosystem of gratitude and reciprocity, where each entity is motivated to contribute. This cycle of positive actions results in a supportive network that is incredibly powerful in building a successful, sustainable business.

10.4. Trust: The Pillar of Sustainable Relationships

Sustainable relationships pivot on a crucial element: trust. Businesses not only need to build trust but also maintain it through consistent and honest actions. Demonstrating authenticity and integrity in your dealings helps forge a solid reputation, which is vital to expand your network.

Showing genuine concern for your partners, honoring your commitments, and delivering high-value output fosters faith in you and your business. In turn, this drives partnerships and alliances towards long-term sustainability, creating a network that stands the test of time.

10.5. The Ripple Effect: Your Contribution to the Larger Business Ecosystem

In embracing interdependence and nurturing sustainable relationships, your business extends its impact beyond immediate connections. Each responsible step you take creates a ripple effect within the business world, setting higher benchmarks, and inspiring others to adopt equitable, sustainable practices.

As Buddha taught, we do not exist in isolation. Every thought, action, or business decision we make influences the collective thread of life. When we uphold values of interdependence, mutual benefit, generosity, understanding, and trust, we ultimately contribute to a healthier, more balanced, and prosperous business ecosystem.

In conclusion, emphasizing interdependence and adopting Buddha's teachings can infuse your networking strategy with mindfulness and depth. Steered by these timeless principles, your business becomes capable of forging sustainable, high-value relationships that yield substantial growth while contributing positively to the larger corporate landscape. These values transform networking from a mere business necessity into a purpose-driven endeavor, aligning our professional pursuits with the path of empathy, harmony, and collective prosperity.

Chapter 11. Enlightenment in Action: Case Studies of Conscious Businesses

Times are changing, and the business world is evolving at an unprecedented pace. Yet, amidst the flurry of tech innovation and changing business doctrines, a new light emerges from the wisdom of the past. By revisiting the profound teachings of Buddha and integrating them with business operations, we unveil a sustainable business blueprint rooted in the ethos of love, mindfulness, and shared prosperity. Enlightened enterprises draw from these ageless wisdoms to foster conscious and enhanced business practices which are both socially responsible and economically sustainable.

11.1. Path to Enlightenment: Bearaby and Mindful Management

Enter Bearaby, a for-profit social enterprise that embodies Buddha's teachings to the core. Bearaby produces artisanal, hand-knitted weighted blankets that deliver wellness without wreaking havoc on the environment. It is a company that indeed demonstrates how Buddha's doctrine of the virtuous Right Livelihood—making a living without inflicting harm—is applicable to today's business practices.

Bearaby's mantra to deliver wellness to consumers recognizes their responsibility to the planet. Using sustainably sourced raw materials, a biodegradable and compostable fabric known as TENCEL Lyocell is used in crafting their napper blanket. They eschew the use of artificial fillers in favor of more eco-friendly materials, which means that their products are crafted with mindfulness and respect for the environment.

Bearaby further practices the Buddha's teachings of Right Intention and Right Speech in their transparent communication about how the products are manufactured, the environmental footprint, and their commitment to social responsibility, clearly displayed on their website and shared publicly. The brand nurtures trust and authentic relationships with customers by maintaining honest and clear communication—a demonstration of enlightenment in action.

11.2. Reviving Traditions: Threads 4 Thought and Conscious Consumerism

Threads 4 Thought, a clothing retailer headquartered in the fashion capital of New York, liberates fashion from the clutches of fast fashion and environmental degradation. Their business model weaves together Buddha's teachings of Right Mindfulness and Right Concentration, expressing commitment to sustainability, fair labor, and community development.

Their mindful selection of environmentally-friendly materials such as organic cotton, recycled polyester, and Lenzing's Modal—a carbon-neutral fabric derived from beechwood trees—illustrates the conscious choice to protect the environment, and by extension, all beings dwelling within it.

Threads 4 Thought's concentration on fair labor aligns with Buddha's teaching of 'karuna' or compassion—one of the four Sublime States in Buddhism. They employ third-party audits and certifications to ensure that their factories uphold fair, safe, and clean working conditions. Moreover, they contribute to community development by supporting and engaging with community programs in places of their operation.

11.3. The Enlightened Plate: Purple Carrot and Compassionate Commerce

Purple Carrot, a plant-based meal delivery service, superbly embodies Buddha's teachings of Right Action and Right Livelihood. Recognizing that the meat industry is a considerable driver of greenhouse gas emissions, deforestation, and water pollution, Purple Carrot took decisive action.

Their plant-forward meals epitomize Right Action, offering consumers the choice to opt for food that is beneficial to both the individual and the planet. Through their delivery service, they offer healthy, eco-friendly meals directly to consumers, without compromising on taste and nutritional value. By making plant-based eating easier and attractive, they are encouraging environmentally supportive eating habits.

Designing a successful enterprise on principles of compassion and sustainability, Purple Carrot stands testament that enterprises can be profitable while effectively mitigating social and environmental harm. This demonstrates the potency of the Buddha's teachings, or 'dharmas,' in driving compassionate commerce and conscious consumption in the modern world.

Bearaby, Threads 4 Thought, and Purple Carrot: these three businesses, each in their sector, lead by example, showcasing the true potential of an enlightened business approach that merges ancient wisdom and modern business acumen. As they continue to progress on their journey, they reinforce the truth that the Buddha's wisdom is timeless and fully applicable in today's world. By embodying these teachings, we can bring about a profound revolution: creating a marketplace that thrives on consciousness, compassion, and mutual prosperity.

Through conscious choices, we can redefine the parameters of success to reflect not only financial returns but also societal and environmental impact. With enlightenment in action, the future of business seems resplendent with promise, purpose, and collective prosperity. With Buddha's wisdom as our guiding beacon, the age of the conscious entrepreneur has indeed dawned.

www.ingramcontent.com/pod-product-compliance
Lightning Source LLC
Chambersburg PA
CBHW071035260726
48661CB00007B/3035